The Trinity

Morne Campher

Published by Morne Campher, 2022.

While every precaution has been taken in the preparation of this book, the publisher assumes no responsibility for errors or omissions, or for damages resulting from the use of the information contained herein.

THE TRINITY

First edition. December 11, 2022.

Copyright © 2022 Morne Campher.

ISBN: 979-8215024584

Written by Morne Campher.

Also by Morne Campher

Wisdom For Everyday
The Spirit Filled Life
Food For Thought
My True Identity
The Trinity

Table of Contents

Thanksgiving

I have to thank my heavenly Father. He gave me the idea for this devotional, He gave me the ability to write and He sent people with various skills and the know-how my way. He opened the doors for me. He made a way where there seemed to be no way.

I also want to thank my pastor, Wimpie Helmand. Whenever I had any theological questions, he was ready to answer them. Wimpie also contributed financially to the recordings of these devotionals. Furthermore, he also encouraged me to have this book published. Karen Loots organised for these devotionals to be broadcast on community radio stations and she also planned for these devotionals to be recorded. Adrian Lange gave me permission to use a vision he had as an illustration story. Sandra (Soekie) Krog gave me permission to use one of her illustrations as an illustration story.

A New Way Of Living

"And for this reason He [Jesus] is the Mediator of the new covenant, by means of death, for the redemption of the transgressions under the first covenant, that those who are called may receive the promise of the eternal inheritance."

Hebrews 9: 15 (NKJV)

When two or more parties agree on something, they sign a contract. The contract stipulates the role each party has to perform. A covenant is more binding than that. It is very legal. It is binding. It is everlasting.

God made a covenant with mankind. He swore an oath to Himself, seeing that there was no higher authority to do so. He stipulated how He was going to deal with man. The new covenant He made is based on grace and not on performance. The way man behaves does not influence God's love, grace and mercy for us.

We can trust Him completely. He is true and faithful. He will never break the covenant He has made. The covenant He made is sealed with the blood of Jesus.

The original audience of the letter to the Hebrews were persecuted Jewish Christians. They were very familiar with the law. They knew the requirements. They knew what they had to do. This letter showed them that Christ was not an abandonment of their Jewish roots, but rather a fulfillment of their heritage.

In Genesis, we read about Melchizedek. He was a priest. His priesthood is proof that God had always planned to give His people the new covenant. That does not mean that the law Moses received was just a waste of time. The old covenant had its 'flaws,' but they were intentional.

The old covenant served a purpose. These 'flaws' showed us that we needed a new covenant.

When the old covenant was in play, priests had to sacrifice animals to atone for the sins of the nation. They also had to cleanse themselves in order to be in the presence of God. Those animal sacrifices were limited. They could not really remove the penalty of sin. However, Christ is the perfect Lamb of God. His Blood paid the price for our sin. He also fulfilled all the requirements of the law so that we were made righteous and can be in God's presence.

The new covenant does not only give the Jewish believers their eternal inheritance, but it gives that inheritance to everybody who calls on the Name of the Lord.

When you look into a mirror, you will see your own reflection. If your face has dirt marks on it, the mirror will reflect them also. However, the mirror cannot remove the dirt. In the same way, the old covenant showed what was required to be righteous, but it could not make anybody righteous. Jesus fulfilled every single requirement of the law. He gave His righteousness to all who believe in Him. He sealed the new covenant with His own Blood.

Lord Jesus, You made it possible for me to be with God. You paid the penalty for the sins I committed. You made me righteous. All I can say is, thank you. In Your Name I pray, Lord Jesus. Amen.

A Covenant Sealed With Blood

"Now the blood shall be a sign for you on the houses where you are. And when I see the blood, I will pass over you; and the plague shall not be on you to destroy you when I strike the land of Egypt."

Exodus 12: 13 (NKJV)

The Israelites – God's chosen people – were slaves in the land of Egypt. God sent them a deliverer. Moses was to lead them out of slavery in Egypt to freedom, to the promised land.

Pharaoh (king of Egypt) did not want to let them go. He hardened his heart against God. Same thing today: the world does not want to let people go, it will fight tooth and nail to keep people in bondage.

Nine different plagues came down on Egypt. Each time Pharaoh just hardened his heart and refused to let the Israelites go. The tenth plague would bring death to all the first-born. To avoid the coming death, the Israelites had to cover their doorposts with the blood of a lamb. The lamb was a substitute for their first-born children. Death would then pass over them. When God saw the blood, He would not execute judgement on that particular house.

There can be no deliverance without blood. The Israelites had to apply the blood of a lamb to their doorposts. If they didn't, they would have suffered the same fate as the Egyptians, their first-born would have died. Even though this plague was specifically designed for the Egyptians, the Israelites were also included. Death of the first-born were to come to all in the land of Egypt. The Israelites are descendants of Abraham. God made a covenant with Abraham. Because of this covenant, the Jewish people were a special people. However, their special relationship did not exempt them from what was to come. They had to apply the blood of the Passover lamb. The only difference between the Egyptians and the Israelites were the application of an unblemished lamb's blood.

The Passover was one of the Jewish feasts. This feast commemorated their redemption from Egyptian slavery. Blood was also needed to atone for the sins of the people. However, an innocent lamb had to be sacrificed each year. The blood of a created being can never be good enough as the whole of creation is affected by sin.

Jesus came. He is the perfect Lamb of God. His sacrifice on the cross was enough, once and for all. He redeemed the whole world of their guilt caused by sin. He set people free from slavery to sin, just like the Israelites were freed from the yoke the Egyptians placed on them. Just like the Passover lamb was a substitute for the first-born, Jesus is a substitute for sinful-man.

The blood on the doorposts were a physical sign. Our hearts have been washed clean by the Blood of Jesus. Spiritually, it is a sign showing that we have passed from death to life. Jesus sealed the new covenant with His own Blood.

Place both of your hands in front of you. Both hands are covered with light. However, place a book above one hand. That hand is now covered by the book. The hand is cut off from the light and covered by blackness. That is what sin has caused. It caused people to be separated from the presence of God. The 'sinless' hand is still covered in light. That hand represents Jesus. It is still connected to light. Jesus is our substitute. Instead of sin separating us from God, Jesus took our sin upon Himself and reconciled us with God.

Lord Jesus, thank you for being my Substitute. You have sealed the new covenant with Your Blood. I am free because of You. You are the perfect Lamb of God who takes away the sin of the world. In Your Name I pray, Lord Jesus. Amen.

Grace Through Jesus

"For the law was given through Moses, but grace and truth came through Jesus Christ."

John 1:17 (NKJV)

God gave the Israelites His law in the desert. Moses was the man who received it. Through his ministry, the Israelites gained knowledge of the law. They had to perform.

Thousands of years later, Jesus came. He gave us a new covenant. It is based on both grace and truth. It is available to all who believe in Him. This new covenant was made possible by the finished works of the cross. It has eternal value.

The law pointed out that which was wrong. It showed man his imperfections. It showed man that he could never be with God because everybody is guilty of sin. Jesus came and not only showed us that truth, but He also gave us a way of 'fixing' what was broken. He gave us both truth and grace.

Good deeds alone cannot save a man. Grace, through faith, does that. The very first miracle Moses did was to turn water into blood. That speaks of judgement. Jesus' first miracle was to turn water into wine. The wine symbolises blood. It speaks of grace.

Just before the Israelites left Egypt, they had to cover their doorposts with the blood of a lamb. The lamb's blood covered them from the wrath of God. Only those people who accept Jesus will be spared the judgement that we all deserve.

If God were to to deal with man on the basis of truth alone, we would all perish. We would all be doomed to eternal damnation. That is because all of us have sinned. If He were to deal with us based on grace alone, He would be a liar. That is because Jesus would have had no need to die on the cross and sin would not have been punished.

The Holy Spirit ushered in the new covenant on the day of Pentacost – on the day the outpouring took place. God dealt with the error of man's way. Sin and also made it possible that He could indwell us and be with us forever. The new covenant that Jesus, through His death and resurrection, made possible and started with the outpouring of the Holy Spirit, is based on both grace and truth. Jesus replaced the law of Moses with a focus on the divine revelation.

Comparing a stone with the same-sized sponge leads to an obvious conclusion. The stone is much heavier than the sponge. It is also much harder. That is what the law, the old covenant, is like. It is both a heavy burden and hard. It is impossible to fulfill its requirements. The sponge represents our hearts. God promised the Israelites that there would come a time when He would write the law on their hearts. That time came with the resurrection of Jesus.

Lord Jesus, than you that You dealt with sin. Thank you that You took the punishment that was meant for me. Thank you that You made the new covenant possible. In Your Name I pray, Lord Jesus. Amen.

Finding Life

"who also made us sufficient as ministers of the new covenant, not of the letter but of the Spirit; for the letter kills, but the Spirit gives life."

2 Corinthians 3: 6 (NKJV)

Paul wrote to the Corinthian church that he was confident in his ministry, a confidence he did not get from himself. His authority was not based on his own skill, but on God's authority.

Nothing of value came from himself or his fellow apostles. God made them apostles of the new covenant. He made them sufficient and adequate.

He specifically makes it clear that through the new covenant salvation is obtained from having faith in Christ. It is all based on grace and not through following the law of Moses, as the old covenant required.

Paul, in his old life, was a Pharisee, a minister of the law. He taught people to obey the law of Moses, according to the way the old covenant had required them to do. He taught the letter of the law. In his new role – an apostle of Jesus – he taught people who believed in Jesus to obey the Spirit.

People trying to obey the law, soon finds that it is impossible to do so. The more they try, the more they are aware of their own sin. Sin condemns people to death. The letter of the law brings death. Jesus died on the cross. His death paid the price, the penalty that sin requires. His blood offers forgiveness. The Holy Spirit indwells any person who accepts Jesus as his Lord and Saviour. The Spirit gives life. It is only through the new covenant that we can receive the Spirit, that we can gain life.

Moses went up the mountain to receive the law. The people saw that Moses took a long time to come back. They convinced Aaron to built them a golden calf. They worshipped that image, that calf. However, God was aware of what they did. He sent Moses back down. Moses was angry and separated those who wanted to follow the Lord from the rest. On the very day Moses received the law, 3 000 men died. On the day of Pentacost, the Holy Spirit came on all those who were gathered in the upper room. Peter preached the gospel to those in the streets of Jerusalem. That day, 3 000 people came to believe in Jesus. When Moses received the law, people died. When the Spirit was poured out, people were saved.

Lord Jesus, thank you for the new covenant. In You there is life. You paid the price, the penalty, for my sin. I thank you. In Your Name I pray, Lord Jesus. Amen.

The End Of The Old And The Beginning Of The New

"For Christ is the end of the law for righteousness to everyone who believes."

Romans 10: 4 (NKJV)

The letter to the Roman Christians makes it clear that the law cannot save a person. In this verse, Paul makes it clear that the law was never meant to stand on its own forever, but that it always pointed to Jesus, that He was the end of the law and the beginning of righteousness for everyone who believes in Him.

The purpose of the law (the old covenant) was always to reveal man's unrighteousness. It always intended for man to come to repentance.

The Jews had both a zeal for the Lord and a passion for the law. They wanted to be righteous in their own eyes. However, their view of righteousness differs vastly from the righteousness that God wants from His children. No person can become righteous by trying to keep the law. The more they try, the harder it becomes. It is impossible to follow and meet all the requirements of the law. True righteousness is based on what God has done for us through the finished works of Jesus on the cross and not on man's own effort.

Jesus, through His death and resurrection, ended the old covenant and established the new. He died on the cross and was resurrected. He lived a righteous life. He fulfilled all the requirements of the law. He ended man's dependence on animal sacrifices. He paid the penalty for our sins. He gave His righteousness to all those who believes in Him. He put us in a right standing with God.

Jesus was always the goal of the law and became righteousness for everyone who believes in Him.

A friend of mine had a vision. It was about a guy learning to water ski. He struggled to find his balance on the two skis. Like all those who starts out, this guy leaned forward and pulled on the rope (that was tied to the boat) as if trying to pull the boat closer to him. The skis represent our relationship with God as well as fellowship. The rope represents righteousness. When we pull on the rope we exert a lot of effort, but ultimately that effort is wasted. It does not accomplish anything. Human effort cannot achieve righteousness. A seasoned skier relaxes. He leans back on the rope. Jesus is our righteousness. He has done it. He fulfilled the requirements of the law. We can lean back and relax in that.

Lord Jesus, You are my righteousness. Because of You, I can relax because You have put me in a right standing with God. Thank you Lord Jesus. In Your Name I pray, Lord Jesus. Amen.

Freedom In The New

"Stand fast therefore in the liberty by which Christ has made us free, and do not be entangled again with a yoke of bondage."

Galatians 5: 1 (NKJV)

Legalism and religious thinking would have the Christian believe that grace is not enough, that obeying the law of Moses is also a requirement of salvation. It also implies that grace leads to a carnal lifestyle, that grace is a license to sin.

The Christians in Galatia heard Paul's message. He preached the forgiveness of sins through faith in Jesus. However, a group of Jewish religious leaders also came to them. This group of religious leaders was called the Judaizers. They taught the Galatians that it was good to believe in Jesus, but in order to be truly saved the men had to be circumcised and all of them had to follow the Mosaic law.

However, Paul makes it clear that the law cannot save. It shows people their sinfulness, but does not provide a way out. The law is perfect. It is God's standard. It shows what God requires from us in order to be righteous. However, it cannot make a person righteous and is impossible to follow; it is impossible to attain the standard of the perfect God. Only Jesus saves. He lived a perfect life. There was no sin in Him. He died and rose again. He made us righteous. By believing in Him, we become righteous before God. Sin has been punished.

Trying to live according to the law is to put oneself back into slavery. The law makes people slaves to sin again, while Christ has set us free. Legalism and religious thinking place a very heavy yoke on people. There are too many rules to follow and obey, and even then, it is never good enough. Being a child of God and having a relationship with Him is liberating.

Being obedient to Jesus lets us live a Christian life without having to perform religious rituals and ceremonies, without having to conform to a set of rules and without having to rely on our own human strength.

The Mosaic law enslaves. Christ set us free. We are free to serve others. We are free to follow the leading of the Holy Spirit. We are free from sin. We have the freedom to enjoy the presence of God. Jesus set us free so that we may become children of God. There is absolutely no need to become a slave again.

The freedom of the new covenant is not the dangerous doctrine that legalism and religious thinking would have us believe. Obeying the law (or at least trying to) leads to an outward display of discipline. Being obedient and following the Spirit, leads to an inward change that will result in an outward change of behaviour. God's perfect law, through the indwelling and working of the Holy Spirit, are being fulfilled in us; we are being transformed into the image of Christ.

In a museum in Newport News, USA, there is a makeshift kayak. This kayak was used in 1966 by a couple to escape the bondage of Cuba and head for the freedom found in the USA. Once they were rescued by the US Coast Guard, a reporter asked the man if it was worth the risk? Laureano answered "We lived in the enormous prison which is Cuba, where one's life is not worth one crumb. Risking death was a million times more attractive than the oppression we lived under." The freedom of the new covenant is a million times more attractive than the yoke of slavery.

Lord Jesus, thank you for the liberty You offered me through the new covenant. You set me free. You gave me life. In Your Name I pray, Lord Jesus. Amen.

Redeemed: Curse Broken

"Christ has redeemed us from the curse of the law, having become a curse for us (for it is written, 'Cursed is everyone who hangs on a tree')."

Galatians 3: 13 (NKJV)

A religious group tried to preach a new doctrine in Galatia. They said that in order to be saved, one needed to follow Jesus as well as the law of Moses.

Using the Old Testament, Paul showed them that to live by faith and to follow the law was not possible. The two could not be reconciled. It was impossible for man to live up to the standards of God's perfect law.

Living under the law is to live under the threat of God's curse by breaking it. Every person has broken the law, for we have all sinned. There is absolutely nothing that any person can do to come out from under that curse, neither can we add anything to what Jesus did for us. The wages of sin is death. In other words, we are all cursed. We all deserve the death penalty. According to the Mosaic law, the sign of a cursed person is that he should hang on a tree. We were all doomed.

However, Jesus came. He bore the full brunt of God's punishment. He took our place. He did what we could not do for ourselves. He became a curse on our behalf. He hung on a tree by having been crucified. There was no other way to lift the curse. It had to be transferred.

Galatians 3: 3 is the good news, the gospel, in a nutshell. Jesus redeemed us. He broke the curse that we were living under. He ushered in the new covenant. Because of Him, we are no longer cursed, but are free.

Think of a glass of water. The water is pure. However, just one drop of cyanide would spoil that whole glass of water. That is what sin does. It prevents a person from living up to the perfect standards of God. The water can be purified. It involves a complicated method of passing and filtering the water through various absorption processes. Jesus absorbed the curse of our sins. He purified us.

Thank you, Lord Jesus, for having become a curse on my behalf. Because of You, I am no longer cursed and separated from God. I am free to be with my Father. In Your Name I pray, Lord Jesus. Amen.

Not By Works, But By Faith

"For as many as are of the works of the law are under the curse; for it is written, 'Cursed is everyone who does not continue in all things which are written in the book of the law, to do them.' But that no one is justified by the law in the sight of God is evident, for 'the just shall live by faith.'

Galatians 3: 10-11 (NKJV)

No one can gain a right standing with God by following the law. Fallen man cannot keep God's perfect law.

The law makes it clear that one has to obey every single thing that is written. By just breaking one of the laws (even unintentionally), one is guilty of breaking all of the laws. Being guilty of one trespass means that one is then disqualified from gaining righteousness. Not only does one fail in the quest for righteousness, but one is then also placed under a curse.

The law was designed by God to point man in the right direction, to point man to Jesus.

Paul quotes a Scripture from Habakkuk: "The righteous shall live by faith." Abraham was counted as being righteous in the book of Genesis. He was righteous because he had faith in God, not because he followed the law. In fact, the law was not even in existence back then. The same principle applied during all those years Israel had kings. It also applies today.

The law and living by faith are two separate things. The one brings a curse, while the other makes man righteous. The law demands of man to perfectly obey it and by breaking just one, man places himself under a curse. Jesus lived the perfect life. He fulfilled all the requirements of the law. Not only did He fulfill all of the requirements of the written law, but He also fulfilled it in the way that He lived. He only spoke the things that He heard from the Father. He lived in such a way that He completely followed and did the will of the Father. Jesus lived His life in utter dependence on His Father. He took the curse that man was under and placed it on Himself. He died as a righteous Man. He then gave that righteousness to man.

It is through faith that we become righteous. By believing that Jesus is the Son of God, that He died on the cross and rose again, that because of what He did we can be forgiven of all our sin (past, present and future) and by accepting Him as our Lord and Saviour, we are placed in a right standing with God. He has justified us. We are the just that live by faith.

Living by faith is not only the first step in a Christian's life, but our whole life is based on that. We are saved through grace, by faith. By continuing to live by faith, we will be moving from glory to glory.

By accepting Jesus as Lord and Saviour, we identify with His death and resurrection. We then start to live the life God has intended for us. We live by grace, through faith and not by the works of the law. We do not live lives based on the merit of man.

Imagine a house without light. It is dark and murky. It is easy to walk into things, to stumble and fall. The lights need to be switched on in order to see clearly. Jesus is the Light of the world. Our faith in Him is the light switch. Corrie Ten Boom (a Holocaust survivor) said that faith is the radar that allows us to see through the fog of reality. It allows us to see those things that the human eye cannot.

Lord Jesus, I gladly confess that You are the Son of God. I believe with all of my heart that You died on the cross and rose again. You lived a righteous life and because of You, I am righteous. You have placed me in a right standing with God. You have set me free. You have made it possible for me to live by faith and not by works or my own effort. Thank you Lord Jesus. In Your Name I pray. Amen.

A New Reality Established

"then He said 'Behold, I have come to do Your will o God.' He takes away the first that He may establish the second."

Hebrews 10: 9 (NKJV)

In his letters to various churches, Paul made it clear that Jesus was the ultimate sacrifice for our sins. The author of the letter to the Hebrew believers builds on that.

The old covenant could not provide the salvation that people needed. God Himself, through the Person of Jesus, provided the needed salvation. Jesus, through His death and resurrection, made the new covenant possible. The new covenant is superior in all and every way. The old covenant was set aside. It was replaced.

The establishment of the new covenant holds certain applications for us as believers. In the old covenant, priests interceded for the sins of people at set times. They sacrificed animals to atone for people's sins. Furthermore, only the high priest could enter the presence of God. Through the new covenant, Jesus became our high priest. That means we can enter God's presence with boldness and confidence. Jesus also intercedes for us continually. People can ask God for forgiveness of sins directly. There is no more need for any religious practices. Because of this new reality, we can have a personal relationship with God. The new covenant allows us to walk by faith. The new covenant is unparalleled.

A man named Mark Roberts lived in the USA. He was once a guest of a Congressman, named John Campbell. As long as he was with the Congressman, he could enter any area that was marked 'reserved for authorized personnel only.' He could enter those areas, not because of who he was, but because of the name of the Congressman. We can enter the presence of God because of Jesus. He opened the door for us. He established a new reality, He made the new covenant possible.

Lord Jesus, thank you for Your sacrifice. You made it possible for me to enter into the presence of God. Thank you Lord. In Your Name I pray, Lord Jesus, Amen.

Glory Uncovered

"unlike Moses, who put a veil over his face so that the children of Israel cold not look steadily at the end of what was passing away, but their minds were blinded. For until this day the same veil remains unlifted in the reading of the Old Testament, because the veil is taken away in Christ."

2 Corinthians 3: 13-14 (NKJV)

Moses went up the mountain to receive the law. He saw the glory of God. His face reflected that and the Israelites were afraid because of that reflection. He had to cover his face.

Just like the glory eventually faded from Moses' face, so does the old covenant. It was always meant to come to an end. It was always going to be replaced by God's grace, available to all who come to Him through faith in Jesus Christ. The glory of God, revealed through Jesus, is eternal. Through faith in Jesus, God receives the death of Jesus on the cross as the payment for our sins and gives us the credit for the sinless, righteous life of Jesus.

Another application of the new covenant having been uncovered is that Paul, unlike Moses, had boldness to represent God to others. He knew that his standing before God was not based on his own performance, but on the finished works of Jesus. He had nothing to fear. He had confidence in the righteousness of Christ. Moses could not be so bold in representing God to the Israelites. He had to cover his face.

Today, we too can go out with boldness and represent God to a fallen world. Our righteousness is based on what Jesus did. He put us in a right standing with God. He revealed God to us. He uncovered the glory of the old covenant and brought in the new. The veil of unbelief has been removed by the Holy Spirit. We are being transformed into the image of Christ.

Staring at the sun can damage the eyes and make a person go blind. However, staring at a person with sunburn does not have the same effect. Moses had to cover his face because the Israelites could not enter into God's presence. Jesus made it possible for us to be in a right standing with God. He uncovered the glory of the old covenant. He lifted the veil.

Lord Jesus, You unveiled the glory of God. You revealed the new covenant. You made it possible for me to be in a right standing with God. Thank you Lord Jesus. In Your Name I pray, Lord Jesus. Amen.

Jesus Is Our High Priest

"But He, because He continues forever, has an unchangeable priesthood. Therefore He is also able to save to the uttermost those who come to God through Him, since He always lives to make intercession for them. For such a High Priest was fitting for us, who is holy, harmless, undefiled, separate from sinners, and has become higher than the heavens; who does not need daily, as those high priests, to offer up sacrifices, first for His own sins and then for the people's, for this He did once for all when He offered up Himself. For the law appoints as high priests men who have weakness, but the word of the oath, which came after the law, appoints the Son who has been perfected forever."

Hebrews 7: 24-28 (NKJV)

Most people today do not consider the issue of priesthood to be a pressing one. However, the implications of Jesus being our High Priest are of tremendous importance.

The priesthood of Jesus will never end in death, unlike the earthly priests. They could only intercede and serve the people while they were alive. The priesthood of Jesus is superior to the Levitical priesthood of the old covenant. Jesus, unlike earthly priests, is not subject to death. Therefore, He is able to serve and offer salvation continuously. He is the heavenly High Priest.

According to the law, only men from the tribe of Levi could be appointed as priests for the Jewish nation. Jesus was a descendant of Judah. Hence, Jesus did not 'qualify' to be a Jewish priest. Psalm 110 refers to Jesus as a priest forever, according to the order of Melchizedek. Melchizedek was a priest of the Most High during the time of Abraham. Scripture indeed makes it clear that a priest did not have to be a Jew. Jesus is the eternal High Priest of all those who believe in Him – and not only for the Jews.

Earthly priests are limited in their priesthood. They obviously die, meaning their priesthood is of a limited duration. Jesus died and rose again. He was exalted to God's right hand. This means that He can offer eternal salvation. He intercedes for us us. His intercession will never end.

Furthermore, Jesus is unique. He is blameless, holy and undefiled. Jesus, even though tempted in every way, was without sin. Earthly priests are not. Jesus is separated from earthly priests, from sinners. Jesus is exalted above the heavens.

The Jewish priests of the old covenant had to make repeated sacrifices. Those sacrifices were not effective in terms of taking away sin. They could only clean the flesh and only lasted for a short period of time. However, Jesus offered up Himself. His sacrifice was efficient. His sacrifice not only cleanses the flesh, but it also takes away the sin of all those who believe in Him. He only needed to sacrifice Himself once and for all. The sacrifice of Jesus penetrates into the innermost being of a person. He perfects those who are being sanctified. Other sacrifices are needed no more. The sacrifice of Christ was efficient. It was once and for all. Through Him, the new covenant was established whereby the Holy Spirit works in the hearts of man.

Earthly priests were human. They had the fallen, sinful nature of man. Jesus is perfect. His perfection includes His incarnation, death, resurrection and ascension. This is what the Scripture means when it says that Jesus has been perfected forever.

Unlike the priests of the old covenant, Jesus was appointed as High Priest with an oath. Psalm110 references this oath formula. It states that "The Lord has sworn and will not change His mind." The passage here in Hebrews underscores the eternal nature of the priesthood of Jesus.

John Howard Griffin was a white man who believed he could never understand the plight of the African American, unless he became one. He darkened his skin with all sorts of medication and stains. He then travelled throughout the American South. His 1959 book, *Black Like Me*, helped numerous white people to understand their fellow black Americans. Jesus is our High Priest who identified with us in every single way.

Lord Jesus, thank you for being my High Priest. You are perfect. You are not limited in any way. You are eternal. Thank you for having identified with me in every way. In Your Name I pray, Lord Jesus. Amen.

A Heavenly Tabernacle

"a Minister of the sanctuary and of the true tabernacle which the Lord erected, and not man."

Hebrews 8: 2 (NKJV)

The priesthood of Jesus is superior and it is in direct connection with the new covenant. Jesus sits at the right hand of God in heaven. He has finished the works of the cross, He has all the power and authority and He is unmatched in being worthy of praise.

Moses received the law. The tent of meeting, or the tabernacle, was the appointed place for God's presence, sacrifices and for worship. The plans for the construction of this temporary building was given by God. All of this was merely a shadow of what was to come. Jesus offered Himself as the perfect sacrifice in the perfect place – an eternal place constructed by God, heaven. The new covenant was always God's plan for the redemption of man.

The tabernacle was a temporary building. It was later replaced by a more permanent building: the temple. Even that was temporary. The temple, all the rituals and all the objects in the temple were real and had value. However, they were merely a shadow of things to come. That is their true worth.

Jesus is our High Priest. His role is superior to the old covenant system, not only because He is the perfect Lamb of God, but also because His sacrifice and service occurs in the true tabernacle. Whereas the old covenant's rituals and sacrifices were repetitive, limited and earthly, God planned for the new covenant to be complete, personal and eternal.

A public minister of holy things in the sanctuary or tabernacle/temple, was the role the Levites had to fulfill. They functioned in an office, performing certain tasks and rituals. They had to offer sacrifices. They officiated for the public. Part of their tasks included the work of prayer and praise. It was designed for the people at large – everybody had the right to attend these, everybody had an equal interest in it. The priest was the servant of the public. He transacted the business of the people with God. He performed his duties in the tabernacle/temple. It was the symbolic place of God's presence.

Jesus performs the same function as our High Priest and Mediator. He transacts the business of the whole human race with God. However, Jesus is not limited to a specific place or building. He is in heaven. Heaven is the place where God dwells in all His glory. It is manifested to all the angels and to the glorified saints. Heaven is the true tabernacle.

The Jewish tabernacle was built by man, but heaven is the work of God alone. It is infinitely more glorious than the Jewish tabernacle. The new covenant reveals to us the true tabernacle.

Going on a camping trip can be a miserable experience, especially if one is not a camper. Pitching a tent can be difficult. It is uncomfortable to stay in. It is very temporary. Even if there are no tents involved, chances are that the dwellings are makeshift shelters. These could 'host' unwanted creepy crawleys. Tents, campers and makeshift shelters are all temporary. People don't expect to live the rest of their lives in these. They are not the real McCoy.

Lord Jesus, You are my High Priest. Thank you that You are not limited to earthly dwellings. You are in heaven. In Your Name I pray, Lord Jesus. Amen.

Saved By Grace Through Faith

"For by grace you have been saved through faith, and that not of yourselves, it is the gift of God."

Ephesians 2: 8 (NKJV)

Adam and Eve fell into temptation. As a result, sin spread throughout the earth.

God destroyed all living things by having send the flood. However, after the flood, sin started to spread again. Eventually, God called Abraham. His descendants would become God's chosen people – the Israelites.

Jacob and his sons moved to Egypt to avoid the famine. They thrived there, but they also became slaves to the Egyptians. God delivered them from their slavery. During their time in the desert, God gave them the law to separate them from all the nations around them.

The law was meant to show them what sin was and how much they needed a Saviour. They had to obey the law. They were given mercy for offering sacrifices for sin and not adopting the practices of the idol-worshipping nations around them. They had to earn their righteousness until the time came when the Messiah would permanently wash away their sin. Foreigners were not excluded from this. They could also earn their righteousness by following the law. People like Rahab and Ruth are examples of foreigners who followed this way of living. However, the law always hung over the people's head's because no one could keep it.

Jesus, the Messiah, came. He took the wrath of God upon Himself. He paid the price for all of mankind's sin – past, present and future. He was the fulfillment of the law, the fulfillment of the old covenant. Today, trust in Jesus is all that is needed. He is the Son of God who paid the price for our sin. If we believe in Him, we are saved.

The new covenant of righteousness is established through faith in Him. No longer are the old covenant needed for the Blood of Jesus was the final sacrifice. We cannot sin beyond Christ's ability to save us. Because of Him, we are free from sin (not free to sin).

The old covenant was only a shadow of the new and better way. Grace is God's part in the salvation plan. Faith in Jesus is our part.

Grace means that God loves, forgives and saves us, not because of what we have done, but because of the finished work of Jesus. God declares us righteous because of what Jesus did. We receive God's grace through faith. Our salvation is not dependent on a do's and don'ts list, but on grace through faith in Jesus.

A shadow is a dull, distorted image of a silhouette that is cast out by the true person. The real person is so much more than what the shadow portrayed. The law, the old covenant, was merely a shadow of Jesus.

Lord Jesus, You fulfilled all the requirements of the law. You paid the price for my sin. You set me in a right standing with God. You made me righteous. Thank you, Lord Jesus. In Your Name I pray. Amen.

Sin: Remembered No More

"then He adds, 'Their sins and their lawless deeds I will remember no more.'"

Hebrews 10: 17

God's plan, all along, was to send Jesus to deal with sin, once and for all. The author of the Hebrew letter quoted from Jeremiah to make that point.

The Holy Spirit inspired the prophet Jeremiah to write about the new covenant. God said that He will bring in a new covenant. This new covenant would be superior to the law given to Moses and administered by the Levitical priests. The old covenant was centred on the priests and the temple. Those practices and objects were symbols of the real cure that was to come. There would be no need any more for regular animal sacrifices. God's commandments would be written on the hearts of people.

God is faithful. He keeps His promises. In Hebrews, He builds on the prophecy of Jeremiah. Not only did He bring about the new covenant, but He also completely and comprehensively dealt with sin – it is not remembered any more. The sacrifice of Jesus was enough for the remission of sin. It is complete. It is finished.

Repeated animal sacrifices could never forgive sin, rather, it was a reminder of sin. The new covenant could actually offer forgiveness. Through the crucifixion of Jesus, sin is forgiven. God accepts the death of Jesus as payment for sin. Through Jesus, mankind is cleansed from the inside. Sin is totally forgiven and not merely covered for a short period of time.

Being forgiven should encourage all Christians to hold on to their faith in the face of persecution.

Louisa Fletcher wrote the poem *Beginning Again*. In it, she writes. I wish there were some wonderful place called "The Land Of Beginning Again," where all our mistakes, and all our heartaches and all of our poor selfish grief could be dropped like a shabby old coat at the door, and never be put on again." Well it does exist. It is the new covenant and because of the sacrifice Jesus, our sins are remembered no more.

Lord Jesus, because of You, I am forgiven. My sins are remembered no more. You paid the price. You fulfilled every requirement and completed my redemption. Thank you. In Your Name I pray, Lord Jesus. Amen.

A Ministry Of Life

"But if the ministry of death, written and engraved on stones, was glorious, so that the children of Israel could not look steadily at the face of Moses because of the glory of his countenance, which glory was passing away, how will the ministry of the Spirit not be more glorious?"

2 Corinthians 3: 7-8 (NKJV)

Paul compares the two covenants between God and His people. He was well qualified to do so. He was a minister of the old covenant, a Pharisee and then became an apostle of Jesus.

As a Pharisee, he served as a minister of the old covenant. He goes on to describe it as the ministry of death. However, he does not dismiss it. After all, it was instituted by God. It was perfect. Instead, Paul shows that purpose of the old covenant was meant to show people their sin and their need for a Saviour. It is impossible for any human to live under the law and to obey it completely. Any transgression results in a person being separated from God and that is punishable by death. Trying to live under the law is the same as living under a death sentence.

In contrast, the new covenant is the ministry of the Spirit. It gives life to those who believe in Christ. There is grace through faith. The new covenant holds far greater glory. Whereas we stood before God as guilty sinners, deserving of death, under the old covenant, we are resurrected with Christ under the new. The new covenant rewards every person with life when they repent. Whereas the old covenant brought condemnation, the new brings righteousness. It outshines the old by far.

As Christians, the new covenant allows us to experience God's presence. We can behold the glory of the Lord. It is all made possible because of the sacrifice of Christ. He is our Mediator and our High Priest. Because of Him, we can enter boldly into the presence of Christ. The Holy Spirit then uses this presence to transform us into the image Christ. We are being transformed by God's glory, for God's glory and into the image of God's glory.

The moon may shine brightly on a clear night. Because of its light, we can see fairly clearly. However, even at its brightest, the moon can never outshine the sun. The old covenant reflected God's glory, but the new positively outshines the old. It not only reflects God's glory, but it also enables us to be righteousness and it gives life.

Lord Jesus, thank you for the new covenant. Thank you for giving me life, and abundantly so. In Your Name I pray, Lord Jesus. Amen.

One Mediator

"For there is one God and one Mediator between God and men, the Man Christ Jesus,"

1 Timothy 2: 5 (NKJV)

Genesis tells us that God created the heavens and the earth. Psalms also tells that the heavens and earth declare His glory. All prayer, praise and worship should be offered to Him. However, sin entered the world. It separated man from God. Mankind was doomed.

God is the only One and True God. That is the foundational belief. Every other belief is tied to that principle belief.

Because sin entered into the world, mankind was forever lost. Doomed to spend all of eternity separated from Him. God does not want any person to be lost. However, He is also just. Sin cannot be in His presence. In terms of eternal life, both God and mankind want the same thing. A third party was needed to bring mankind back to God, to reconcile the two parties. A mediator was needed.

A mediator is an intermediary between two parties, a go-between. That is what Jesus did. His death on the cross ensured that God's righteousness was met by having taken the penalty of sin upon Himself. Because sin has been dealt with, we are now free to enter into God's presence. Through his death, Jesus brought mankind back to God.

It was always God's plan to usher in the new covenant. It was always His plan to bring mankind back to Him. It was always His plan to make His Word the perfect Mediator.

The Word became flesh. Jesus was God in human form. He lived a humiliating life. He suffered greatly at the hands of His own creation.

He died a horrible death. People hated, scorned and mocked Him. Yet, He was also still 100% God. He went through all of that humiliation in order to save mankind. He was the perfect man to have walked the face of the earth. Only Jesus was worthy to become the Mediator between God and mankind.

It is also very important to take in the meaning of the tense in which Paul wrote to Timothy. He described Jesus as the fullness of God in human form. He didn't describe Jesus as having been a man. That means that Jesus is forever our Saviour. He is, as He was back then, fully qualified to be the Mediator between God and man. He shares the nature of both God and man. He is uniquely qualified.

It is through grace that God established the new covenant. It is through faith in Jesus that the new covenant becomes a reality in the lives of all those who have accepted Jesus as their Lord and Saviour.

Angus McGillivray was a Scottish soldier in a prisoner of war camp during the second world war. The prisoners of this camp helped to build the infamous bridge over the river Kwai. Conditions in the camp were horrendous. There was a dog-eat-dog mentality. People stole from each other and cheated one another. The law of the jungle set in. It became all about trying to survive. People in the camp were shocked to hear that Angus had died. He was a big and strong man. His death was not expected.

The Scottish soldiers (also called the Argylls) had a buddy system. Each man would do his utmost to keep his buddy alive. Angus' buddy was one of those men dying. Whenever his buddy got cold, Angus would give him his own blanket. Whenever his buddy was hungry, Angus would give him his own food. As his buddy started to recover and gain strength, Angus became weaker. Angus eventually died, but he saved the life of his buddy.

Jesus too the penalty of our sin upon Himself in order that we may be reconciled with God.

Thank you Lord Jesus for having paid the price for my sin. You made it possible for me to be reconciled with God. You are the Mediator between God and man. In Your Name I pray, Lord Jesus. Amen.

Transforming Our Thinking

"But now He has obtained a more excellent ministry, inasmuch as He is also Mediator of a better covenant, which was established on better promises."

Hebrews 8: 6 (NKJV)

The old covenant was filled with symbolism. It was, however, always God's intention to bring in the new covenant. A covenant that was superior to the old, a covenant to transform the limitations of the old and to transform the hearts and minds of people.

God made known to man His intention of redemption from sin. Redemption that opened the door for salvation to all people. Ultimately, every person would be offered the opportunity to become a part of His family, to be righteous sons and daughters of the Most High.

God has never wavered in His commitment. Every person that believes in Jesus, that accepts Him as Lord and Saviour, has the right to become a child of God. It is through Jesus that people can step into the destiny that God has planned for them. Because of Jesus, God's grace abounds to us. That makes the new covenant a far better one.

The new covenant has better promises. The better promises relate to eternal life. Through the sacrifice of Christ, sin is forgiven and the gift of the Holy Spirit was made possible. The new covenant started the process of transforming the hearts and minds of people who accepted Christ. The new covenant, through Jesus, makes us heirs of an eternal inheritance.

Jesus is far superior to the Levites, the priests of the old covenant. His ministry is never-ending. He fulfills the all the requirements of the new covenant. We reap the benefits. The ministry of Jesus is not a type and neither is it temporary. His ministry is absolute. His ministry is eternal. The promises of the new covenant are spiritual and not limited to earthly circumstances.

People that know me now find it very difficult to believe that I once was the type person who lived in rebellion. I also find it hard to understand the things I used to say and do. Today, I am 180 degrees the opposite of what I used to be. That is all because of Jesus. He transformed me. He gave me eternal life. He is the Eternal Minister of the new covenant. He transforms people. He makes everything new.

Lord Jesus, You saved me. You transformed my life. You are my eternal Priest. To You be all the glory forever and ever In Your Name I pray, Lord Jesus. Amen.

Boldness To Receive Mercy And Grace

"Let us therefore come boldly to the throne of grace, that we may obtain mercy and find grace to help in time of need."

Hebrews 4: 16 (NKJV)

The old covenant was full of symbolism. The ark of the covenant – a golden box containing the written law God gave Moses on two stone tablets – was covered by the mercy seat. The mercy seat was basically a golden lid covering the ark of the covenant. This was placed in the Holy of Holies section of the temple, separated from other areas by a curtain. The temple was the place of God's presence. Only the high priest could enter the Holy of Holies.

Jesus is the central Figure of our faith. He made the new covenant possible. He is not a flawed spirit or being that cannot identify and understand the human nature. Jesus was tempted in every way and overcame them all. He is our High Priest. We can enter into God's presence because of Jesus. Mercy can be found in God's presence.

Because Jesus understands our nature, we can come boldly to God to ask for mercy and grace. Because Jesus is the Lamb of God as well as our High Priest, we can be confident and assured that Jesus understands every situation we go through, every hardship we face and all the pain we experience. We can pray to God with an easiness – not worrying about something we did wrong. It is great reassurance to have.

Jesus is the gracious Son of Man. He is the Saviour. He is also God. He created the whole universe. He is omnipotent. He is merciful, full of compassion and goodness. There is no need to be afraid of God, but a reverence for who He is and what He has done for us is demanded. We cannot help to stand in awe of Him when we realise these things.

This bible verse should fill us with joy. God's throne is an eternal one. It is one of grace. His mercy has covered our sins for all of eternity. Because of Jesus, sin no longer separate us from God — no longer is there a need to separate the Holy of Holies by a veil. Through grace, by faith in Jesus, we have been given access to God's throne.

It is an amazing privilege we have. It is a privilege extended to all people who come to Jesus. Not only is it an invitation, but it is also a reward for believing in Jesus.

God is a God of grace and love, but He is also just and righteous. Sin had to be punished. By His grace, Jesus took the punishment of the whole world's sin upon Himself. By believing in Him, we are forgiven. Not only are we forgiven, but we we are also declared righteous. What grace!

A certain man had a son who died in a war. The son shared his father's love love for the arts. He even painted a scene during a battle before his death. A soldier, who served with the son, gave the father the painting. The father was filled with emotion and joy. He proudly displayed his son's painting among all the valuable art pieces in his collection. Upon the father's death, the art pieces were put on auction. The auction included the painting of the son. The auction opened with the son's painting being the first piece to go under the hammer. However, there was just one bidder for this piece. The bidder was a servant who also loved the son. When he won, he also received a note. The note said 'Whoever buys my son's painting can have all the rest of the paintings too. He who loves my son can have everything I own.'

Jesus died on the cross for us. He rose again. He is alive. He has opened up the way for us to be in God's presence. By accepting Him as our Lord and Saviour, we also get given God's mercy and grace.

Lord Jesus, You died for me. Because of You, I am forgiven and righteous. You made it possible for me to enter the throne room of grace – no longer am I separated from God. Thank you, Lord Jesus. In Your Name I pray. Amen.

All Bases Covered

"Therefore He is also able to save to the uttermost those who come to God through Him, since He always lives to make intercession for them."

Hebrews 7: 25 (NKJV)

"Now He who searches the hearts knows what the mind of the Spirit is, because He makes intercession for the saints according to the will of God."

Romans 8: 27 (NKJV)

Interceding for the Israelites was one of the duties of the old covenant priests.

The death and resurrection of Jesus made the new covenant possible. The new covenant began with the outpouring of the Holy Spirit.

To intercede for someone means to plead on another person's behalf. Jesus is pleading with God for our salvation. Jesus intercedes for us because God is Holy. Sin has not lost its seriousness, even though Jesus died to pay the penalty for our sin. Those people who trust in Jesus are safe. He specifically point to an event in history: His own sacrificial death. His death paid the price for our sin. His death set us free. His death made us righteous. His death put us in a right standing with God. That is the case He pleads before God.

It is not as if He has to persuade God, and neither does God hate us. He is simply pointing out that He has paid the price – a price that was required to satisfy God's righteous judgements and requirements. The devil accuses us night and day. Jesus points to His own sacrifice. That counters whatever argument the devil can make.

God knows our hearts, our longings for Him and our desire for Him. We are not able to express these in words. However, the Holy Spirit indwells every child of God. He knows exactly what is in the hearts of every believer. In turn, God knows the mind of the Spirit. God knows precisely what is in the hearts of His children (even if we don't know our own hearts exactly) because the Spirit intercedes for us. God knows the thoughts of the Spirit.

Baseball requires a person to hit a ball and run to a series of bases before returning 'home' and scoring a run. When batter A starts off on his run, he may need several other batters to step up to the plate before he can return home and score his run. Jesus and the Holy Spirit intercedes for us. All our bases are covered. We are assured of scoring – our eternal life is secured and we are also covered in prayer while we walk this earth.

Lord Jesus, You made the new covenant possible. I am secure in You. Thank you for interceding for me, for pleading my case. Your death paid the price for my guilt. Thank you Holy Spirit for knowing my heart. Thank you that You know exactly what is going on in my heart, even if I can't express myself properly. Thank you for interceding for me. In Your Name I pray Lord Jesus. Amen.

Proper Discernment

"But we know that the law is good if one uses it lawfully,"

1 Timothy 1: 8 (NKJV)

The law did not come to an end. The law is God's standard. What did change is the way in which it should be applied.

Timothy was Paul's spiritual son. He was to lead the church at Ephesus. False doctrine found its way into the church. A message was proclaimed saying that Jesus was not enough for salvation, but that true salvation lay in keeping every single command of the law, keeping the law perfectly, performing the requirements of the law, following a set of rules that told them what to do and what not to do.

Paul (Saul at the time) knew the Jewish culture and religion. He studied under a Jewish teacher. He was a Pharisee. His life centred around the law. He then converted to Christianity and became an apostle of Jesus. It is in his office as an apostle that he writes to Timothy.

Paul says to Timothy that the law is good if it used in a legitimate manner. The law, used in the proper way, makes people aware of sin, judgement and their need for a Saviour. This is the same role the Holy Spirit fulfills under the new covenant. However, if the law is used illegitimately, it only becomes legalism.

In order to apply the law in its proper way, one must allow the Scriptures to interpret themselves. The Scriptures become the guideline for the application of the law. Our own feelings, opinions and reasoning do not play any part in it. The Bible interprets the Bible. Through the Holy Spirit, the Scriptures become 'alive.'

All Christians need guidance. Scripture itself tell us how that guidance should be given and applied. There are various ministries and gifts within the church. All of them are meant to build each member up and to equip them for ministry. All of Scripture is "profitable for doctrine, for reproof, for correction and for instruction in righteousness."

The old covenant law, when used correctly, encourages sinners to turn to God for the forgiveness of their sins. Under the new covenant, forgiveness of sin is given to all who come through faith to Jesus.

When a dispute over a legal document arises, the various parties will settle the dispute in a court of law. One of the first things the court will do, is to go through the legal document. That document is written in a legal language. It is very strict and difficult to understand. Only a few people do. However, even though the language is difficult, the law does allow itself to be interpreted. Lawyers will make different arguments and quote various case studies. In other words, the law allows itself to be interpreted by itself.

Both the Old Testament and the New Testament make up the Bible. The Bible is God's written Word. The Holy Spirit enables the children of God to interpret the Scriptures.

Thank you, Holy Spirit, for indwelling me. Thank you that You open up the Scriptures to me and enable me to understand them. In Jesus Name I pray. Amen.

A Solid, Unmovable, Unshakable, Absolutely Credible And True Witness

"But The Holy Spirit also witnesses to us; for after He had said before, 'This is the covenant that I will make with them after those days, says the Lord: I will put My laws into their hearts, and in their minds I will write them,'"

Hebrews 10: 15-16 (NKJV)

God knew that people needed to be forgiven of their sins. However, He also wanted His people to realise that they needed salvation.

The old covenant contains more than 600 laws. God's blessing on Israel was dependent on them keeping those laws. They had to perform in order to be blessed. God's blessing, under the old covenant, was conditional.

The letter to the Hebrews was written to persecuted Jewish Christians. They knew the law. The author of the letter to the Hebrews, quoted passages from the Old Testament in order to explain the establishment of the new covenant. Through these quotations, these persecuted Jews could see that God always intended for the new covenant to come into effect. The old covenant was a symbol of the new, meant to teach and prepare people.

All Scripture is inspired by the Holy Spirit. Through Old Testament prophets, He predicted that a time would come where He would write God's law on the hearts of the followers of His people. God's own Words proclaimed His intention to replace the old covenant with a new one.

The author of Hebrews quoted from Jeremiah, attributing the words of the prophecy to be the words of the Holy Spirit. He further says that the Holy Spirit testifies to us about the new covenant. The Holy Spirit is the Witness to the covenant that God established with all people. The

Holy Spirit is proof of the truth, of the fact that Jesus paid the price of sin once and for all, of the fact that because of the sacrifice of Jesus, the new covenant was made possible.

Jesus fulfilled all of the Old Testament prophecies about Him, fulfilled all of the requirements of the law and fulfilled all of the symbols of the priests, the tabernacle and animal sacrifices. The witness of the Holy Spirit is not deception. He is the Spirit of truth. He is infallible. His is the highest authority.

Guests at a wedding are more than mere guests. They are witnesses of a union between two people. We (Christians) are the Church. The church is the Bride of Christ. The Holy Spirit is the witness.

Sometimes, a legal document requires additional signatures – not just those of the parties involved. Those additional signatures are the signatures of witnesses. The Holy Spirit is the witness that God made a new covenant with all people. God Himself is the Witness of the new covenant He established.

Holy Spirit, thank you that You are the Witness of the new covenant. You are the Spirit of truth. Lord Jesus, thank you for Your sacrifice. You made this new covenant possible. In Your Name I pray, Lord Jesus. Amen.

A Personal Relationship

"For this is the covenant that I will make with the house of Israel after those days, says the Lord: I will put my laws in their mind and write them on their hearts; and I will be their God, and they shall be My people."

Hebrews 8: 10

The author of the Hebrew letter continues to quote from Jeremiah, pointing out that God Himself promised to give people a new covenant.

Jesus paid the price for all of mankind's sin. His sacrifice made the new covenant possible. The new covenant is not based on obedience to an external set of legalistic rules, but on an internal personal experience with God. The drive and desire to be obedient to God comes from the inside and is the result of the Holy Spirit working in the lives of God's children. It is the internal nature of the Holy Spirit in the life of a believer.

In the old covenant, people had a mediator. A good example is Moses. He represented them to God and relayed to them the words that God spoke. Because of the sacrifice of Jesus, we now have direct access to God. We can speak to Him directly without fear or hesitation. People can now have a personal relationship with their Father. No longer is revelation required from a third person, but God Himself reveals Himself directly to His children.

God is our God, not in the sense that God is God of all mankind, but He is personal. He is the God of all grace. He is the God of Christ. We are the elect of Christ and are in Him. He is our Father because the new covenant has made it possible for us to be His children. He provides for us. He has set His heart on us. He saves, justifies and sanctifies us, through Jesus. He has adopted us into His family. He is everything implied by the name "God."

We are His people, not as a fact, but as a privilege. We belong. We are counted among those who are special to God, who receives His blessing and whom He calls friends.

Deer are creatures of consistency. They know their territory. They know where to find good food and water. Their constant travels to these sources can be seen in the paths they have created through the wilderness. It only ends when they are driven from their territory. During this time of bewilderment, they start to dehydrate. They long for a sip of water from their familiar source, but also know that danger lurks when they leave the protection of the thickets in which they hide.

People also long for God – even if they do not recognise it as such. Our thirst and hunger can only be satisfied by being in a relationship with Him.

Lord Jesus, thank you for Your sacrifice. You have made it possible for me to be a child of God. Because of You, God is my God. In Your Name I pray, Lord Jesus. Amen.

Knowing Jesus

"None of them shall teach his neighbour, and none his brother, saying 'Know the Lord,' for all shall know Me, from the least of them to the greatest of them."

Hebrews 8: 11 (NKJV)

Jeremiah's prophecy about the new covenant contains many truths. The author of Hebrews expands on them.

Hebrews makes it clear that God intended from the beginning to bring the new covenant into effect. Whereas the old covenant focussed on the following and obedience of an external set of rules, the focus of the new covenant is on the internal. People can now have a personal relationship with God. Jesus, through accepting His sacrifice, offers complete forgiveness of sins and an eternal and personal relationship with God.

We can know God through His Word. However, Jesus died and rose again. Because of that, we have the Holy Spirit indwelling us. We can now know God because of the experiences we have. We can now know Him on a more personal level. We can get intimate knowledge of who Jesus is. Our knowledge is now not merely academic.

Jesus made everything possible. Everyone who accepts Him as Lord and Saviour, will know God. There will be no distinction. Men, women and children will know Him. Rich and poor will know Him. There is no distinction of rank or age. The greatest and the least will know Him. No one is excluded from knowing Jesus. No group has a monopoly on the knowledge of Christ.

There is no need for any intellectual explanations of who God is. Doctrine has become fact. What the prophets in the Old Testament longed for, has been bestowed on us. The Holy Spirit indwells us. We are in a living relationship with our God. We know Jesus. We know what He did. We understand why it was necessary for Him to die in order to save mankind.

We (Christians) are the brothers and sisters of Christ. Because of the sacrifice of Jesus, we will know the Lord. This speaks of the indwelling of the Holy Spirit. He is our Guide and Teacher. He always shows us what Jesus did and what it means for us today.

Instead of mere hearsay, the Holy Spirit in us has brought us to an intimate knowledge of God, to an intimate knowledge and appreciation of what Jesus did. The Holy Spirit works in us to want to know Jesus more and more. The Holy Spirit transforms us into the likeness of Christ.

It may be good to read books about the various wonderful places to travel to, or to watch programmes about them. However, it is entirely different to experience these first-hand. The one is based on hearsay and the other on intimate knowledge. The old covenant taught people about God, but the new covenant brings us into a relationship with Him, into an intimate knowledge of Him. We can truly and honestly say "more of You, Lord Jesus!"

Lord Jesus, thank you for the new covenant. Thank you that I can get to know You. I want to know You more and more, Lord Jesus. You are wonderful. In Your Name I pray, Lord Jesus. Amen.

Everlasting Kindness

"For the mountains shall depart and the hills be removed, but My kindness shall not depart from you, nor shall My covenant of peace be removed,' says the Lord, who has mercy on you."

Isaiah 54: 10 (NKJV)

Israel was heading for captivity due to their own actions, yet God still encouraged them.

Adam sinned and caused the fall of man. Israel came into being. They were God's chosen people. Yet, they too rebelled and backslid. However, God never stopped loving them. Today, because of the new covenant, the Church is God's chosen people. He will never turn His back on the Church.

Mountains and hills symbolise everything mankind see as permanent. However, they will all pass. God's everlasting kindness, on the other hand, is steadfast. His love will always remain. His love is everlasting. The covenant, made and sealed with the Blood of the Lamb, will stand. It cannot be revoked and will never fade away.

God will never leave us nor forsake us. His love for us is unshakable. It is unconditional. Kindness is part of who He is. We can depend on Him. Even when everything around us fail, His loving kindness will not.

God proved His love for us by having sent Jesus to pay the price for our sins. He did so even before we turned to Him for salvation. His death and resurrection and the outpouring of the Holy Spirit made the new covenant possible. Through this new covenant, we can experience God's lovingkindness for ourselves. The love God has for us is evident through Jesus Christ.

Eureka is a TV show on the Sy-Fy channel. It is about a sheriff in a town of geniuses. He often has to work his way through comedic situations. However, his biggest dilemma is Zoe, his daughter. She has been starved of love and long for it. In one episode, she steals someone's credit card and uses it. When her father caught her, she said "I thought that was it. I thought you were done with me." The sheriff replied "Zoe, you are my daughter. I could never be 'done' with you." That response changed her character.

God is never 'done' with us. He loves us. His love is steadfast.

Lord, thank you for Your Love, for Your everlasting kindness. Thank you for not leaving me to my own devices. In Jesus Name I pray. Amen.

A Covenant Of Peace

"For the mountains shall depart and the hills be removed, but My kindness shall not depart from you, nor shall My covenant of peace be removed,' says the Lord, who has mercy on you."

Isaiah 54: 10 (NKJV)

In spite of dire circumstances, we can count on God's covenant – a covenant of peace.

Everything in the world is temporary. Kingdoms rise and fall. Even people we trust and depend on may let us down. Nothing lasts forever.

Sometimes, everything just seems to be overwhelming. However, in spite of how things may appear, God's covenant of peace will never fail because it was made by the Blood of Jesus. We can count on God. He is true. He has made a covenant with us. He is true to His Word. Peace is the result of the Holy Spirit indwelling His people.

God's intention, right from the very beginning, was always to bring in the new covenant. This covenant was made possible because of what Jesus did. Peace is part of the character of God. That characteristic is reflected in the new covenant.

God is from everlasting to everlasting. When all else fails, the peace of God will remain. His children can experience peace in spite of their circumstances. God's people may face adversity, they may be knocked down, they may suffer persecution, but the peace of God will always be in their hearts.

The peace of God is stronger than the visible parts of creation. The visible may be removed, but God will not break His covenant. His covenant does not suffer the consequences and shocks of human and natural events. Even on the last day, when all things will pass away, the people who are part of the new covenant will continue into life everlasting.

A woman went shopping at a mall during the festive season. Her patience was tested. People cut elbowed her out of the way. Somebody even tried to yank a table cloth out of her hands. Later on, she met some friends for tea. She was really looking forward to that cup, to just relax. However, her waitress was rude and told her to "wait her turn." A young man then came over to her table, introduced himself and told her that he would be their waiter. He even helped the rude waitress with a tray she had to carry. In spite of all the crowds, in spite of all the demands, in spite of all the pressures placed on the staff, he remained calm. He was a child of God. He is a good example of what the peace of God can do.

Father, thank you for Your peace. Thank you that I can remain calm in all circumstances because You are. In Jesus Name I pray. Amen.

God Of Mercy

"For the mountains shall depart and the hills be removed, but My kindness shall not depart from you, nor shall My covenant of peace be removed,' says the Lord, who has mercy on you."

Isaiah 54: 10 (NKJV)

By definition, mercy is to withhold judgement.

We are sinners. We deserved death as punishment for our sins. However, God took our sins upon Himself in the Person of Jesus. He granted us forgiveness – something we could never have earned. Not only did he withhold our deserved punishment, but He also gave us what we didn't deserve. He declared us righteous. Because of what Jesus did, we are in a right standing with God. This is the God that made the new covenant.

God will rebuke both the individual Christian as well as the corporate body – the Church. He will correct His people, but He will not cast them aside.

God established the new covenant based on His mercy and not on our own merits. The fulfillment of the covenant terms depend on Him and not on us. He is slow to anger and swift to show mercy. He will gather His people on the last day and show them mercy. His mercy is from everlasting to everlasting.

A story is told of the mayor of New York in 1935. A person named H. La Guardia. He showed up at a night court, dismissed the judge and presided over a case involving a woman who stole bread so that her grandchildren would have had something to eat. He told the woman that he had to punish her. The fine was $10. He threw $10 of his own money into his hat and passed the hat around. He fined every person present that evening 50 cents for 'living in a city where a woman has to steal bread to feed her grandchildren.' The woman left the courtroom, the fine having been paid and having an extra $47,50.

Father, thank you for Your mercy. Thank you Lord Jesus for having paid the penalty for my sin and for having made me righteous. In Your Name I pray, Lord Jesus. Amen.

Undeserved Abundance

"For you know the grace of our Lord Jesus Christ, that though He was rich, yet for your sakes He became poor, that you through His poverty you might become rich."

2 Corinthians 8: 9 (NKJV)

This verse in no way supports the 'name it, claim it and frame it' theory. It means so much more.

The full Godhead of the Triune God dwelt in Christ, all the eternal attributes of God. All things were made for Him and by Him. All the bountiful resources of the vast universe belongs to Him. All the riches of the earth is His possession. He was clothed in majesty before the cross. He had an elevated heavenly status.

In His grace, He left it all behind. He set aside all the riches of heaven and came to earth. He stripped Himself of everything and was born into a fallen, death-ridden, sinful world that had rebelled against its Creator, a world that was in bondage to the devil. He became poor so that the new covenant could be established and all men who believe in Him could be saved.

There were Christians in Jerusalem who suffered. The church in Corinth had made an earlier commitment to help these Christians. They wanted to meet the needs of those Christians. In fact, they had begged Paul for an opportunity to help. Paul reminded them of their pledge.

Paul makes it clear to them that it was not a command to do so, that they did it out of their own free will. It was an opportunity for them to express the love of Christ to fellow believers. He goes on to say that their giving was Christlike. Their giving reflected the nature of Christ – He left all His riches behind to meet the need of man, to become the Saviour of the world. Jesus became willingly poor so that Christians everywhere could become eternally rich.

In 1813, king Frederick William III of Prussia was caught up in a war. He tried to build his nation, but the war was very costly. He did not have the finances to sustain the war effort and capitulating to the enemy was not an option. He made a plan. He asked all the women to exchange their gold jewellery for pieces of iron or bronze. The response was overwhelming. All the women did so. That is what Jesus did for us. He gave up everything so that we might be saved.

Lord Jesus, You gave up everything for me. You became poor so that I could become rich. Thank you Lord. In Your Name I pray, Lord Jesus. Amen.

Shame For Glory

"For it was fitting for Him, for whom are all things and by whom are all things, in bringing many sons to glory, to make the captain of their salvation perfect through sufferings."

Hebrews 2: 10 (NKJV)

Just like Adam and Eve tried to hide from God and covered themselves with fig leaves, sin has separated us from God and brought about shame.

However, Jesus, God incarnate, came to earth. He is the Creator, but He suffered at the hands of His own creation. He satisfied God's righteous need to punish sin. He paid the penalty for our sin and became sin. He was the perfect sacrificial Lamb of God. He is our Saviour. He is the Author and Finisher of our salvation.

Even though Jesus was fully God, He still had to be made perfect through suffering and obedience to the Father. Our incarnate God came to serve. He set the example for us. By doing so, Jesus became the founder of our salvation. He is the captain of salvation. He pioneered the way. He is the Trailblazer and leads the way. His resurrection broke the bonds of slavery. He made the new covenant possible.

That is not where it ends. He was also raised from the dead again. Just like He died, we (Christians) also died to sin, to our old nature. Just like He was raised from the dead, so we too will be raised with Him. Through the new covenant that Jesus made possible, our shame, caused by sin, will be turned into glory.

Moreover, Jesus brought many people to glory by restoring them to God. Because of His death and resurrection, we are adopted as sons and daughters into God's family. He redeemed us for He was the perfect

Man. He lived in total obedience to the Father. He walked in Spirit and truth.

A pastor told the story of his twin daughters going to school. He was excited to see them grow up, but was also dreading it a bit. He knew they would get grades. He also knew that one daughter would get better grades than the other. It filled him with sadness to think that one daughter may feel shame because of lesser grades. He loved both of them. His love for them is not tied to them performing academically. They will always be his daughters, irrespective of their grades.

Lord Jesus, thank you that You made it possible for me to be adopted into God's family. You turned my shame into glory. In Your Name I pray, Lord Jesus. Amen.

The Old Covenant Fulfilled

"Do not think that I came to destroy the law or the prophets. I did not come to destroy but to fulfill."

Matthew 5: 17 (NKJV)

The Ten Commandments are not to be despised. The gospel did not set them aside. It is God's eternal measure of right and wrong.

The Spirit uses the law to show us that we need Jesus, our Saviour, for we cannot keep the law perfectly. Through the law, we become aware of sin and its consequences. Jesus fulfilled all the requirements of the law. He perfectly lived up to the standard of the law.

Jesus is the Word of God incarnate. That includes the law. All of Scripture points to Him, even if there is no direct prophecy about Him. Scripture is unlocked by the death and resurrection of Jesus. He accomplished what the law required – something no man could ever do. The penalty of sin was paid by Him because He lived the perfect life. Only He could do that. Because He paid the price, He is now the way to a righteous life. That was the purpose of the old covenant: look to Jesus; He is the way to righteous living and not trying to keep the law.

No longer are animal sacrifices needed to cover sin. It has been dealt with by the Blood of the perfect Lamb. His sacrifice was efficient to deal with sin once and for all. All who come to Him by faith is forgiven. They are eternally free from the bondage of sin.

The old covenant had many priests. They were meant to be a go-between between the people and God. However, their office was limited. They were subject to death, bringing an end to their service. Jesus lives forever. He is our High Priest. There is no end to His priesthood.

During the Old Testament, the Israelites had a physical temple. It was the symbol of God's presence. Today, every Christian is the temple of the Holy Spirit. He indwells us. Jesus, by His death and resurrection, made it possible for us to be in God's presence.

Jesus fulfilled the ceremonial law. He became the sacrifice that dealt with sin. He fulfilled the moral law by living in complete obedience. Jesus fulfilled the old covenant requirements. He is the Way, the Truth and the Life.

A chicken lays an egg. That egg is an embryo. It has the potential to develop into a full-grown chicken. The old covenant is the embryo of Christianity. Jesus fulfilled it. There is no longer a need to point to something better. Jesus established the new covenant. Through Him, God's glory is reflected. The Spirit transforms us into the image of Christ.

Lord Jesus, You perfectly fulfilled the whole law. You made me righteous. Thank you Lord Jesus. In Your Name I pray, Lord Jesus. Amen.

A Covenant For All

"Likewise He also took the cup after supper, saying 'This is the cup of the new covenant in My Blood, which is shed for you.'"

Luke 22: 20 (NKJV)

In the Old Testament, an agreement or treaty involved rituals of blood sacrifices. God had this type of a covenant with Israel. He gave them the law of Moses. That was the basis on which He dealt with the Israelites. That covenant was sealed with the blood of various sacrificed animals.

Jesus, at the Last Supper, told His disciples that the cup of wine was symbolic of His Blood. It was His Blood that formed the basis of the new covenant. His Blood sealed the agreement. Unlike the old, which was only available to the Israelites, this new covenant is open to all. It is through belief in Jesus that the new covenant is being applied to us. His Blood is enough payment for sin. The Blood of Jesus is sufficient for the atonement of sin. He is the perfect Lamb of God.

The old covenant was a conditional agreement between God and the Israelites. They had to live by various laws, perform certain rituals and keep a number of ceremonies. That was meant to set them apart from the other nations. The new covenant extends God's salvation to all people. Forgiveness of sin is made possible through the sacrifice of Jesus.

To attend a sporting event, one needs a ticket. There are numerous reasons why one may not have a ticket One of them may be the price of the ticket. However, if someone else buys pays for you to attend, it is no longer a problem. That is what Jesus did. The price for our sin was too high. No human could ever pay that price. Jesus did and because of Him, we can enter into the new covenant of God.

Lord Jesus, You paid the price for my sin. You set me free. You made it possible for me to enter into God's presence. Thank you, Lord Jesus. In Your Name I pray, Lord Jesus. Amen.

Don't miss out!

Visit the website below and you can sign up to receive emails whenever Morne Campher publishes a new book. There's no charge and no obligation.

https://books2read.com/r/B-A-ERNU-GINDC

BOOKS2READ

Connecting independent readers to independent writers.

Also by Morne Campher

Wisdom For Everyday
The Spirit Filled Life
Food For Thought
My True Identity
The Trinity

About the Author

Morne Campher was a missionary for seven years. He has a passion for the lost and a desire to see every believer walk in a closer and more intimate relationship with God.